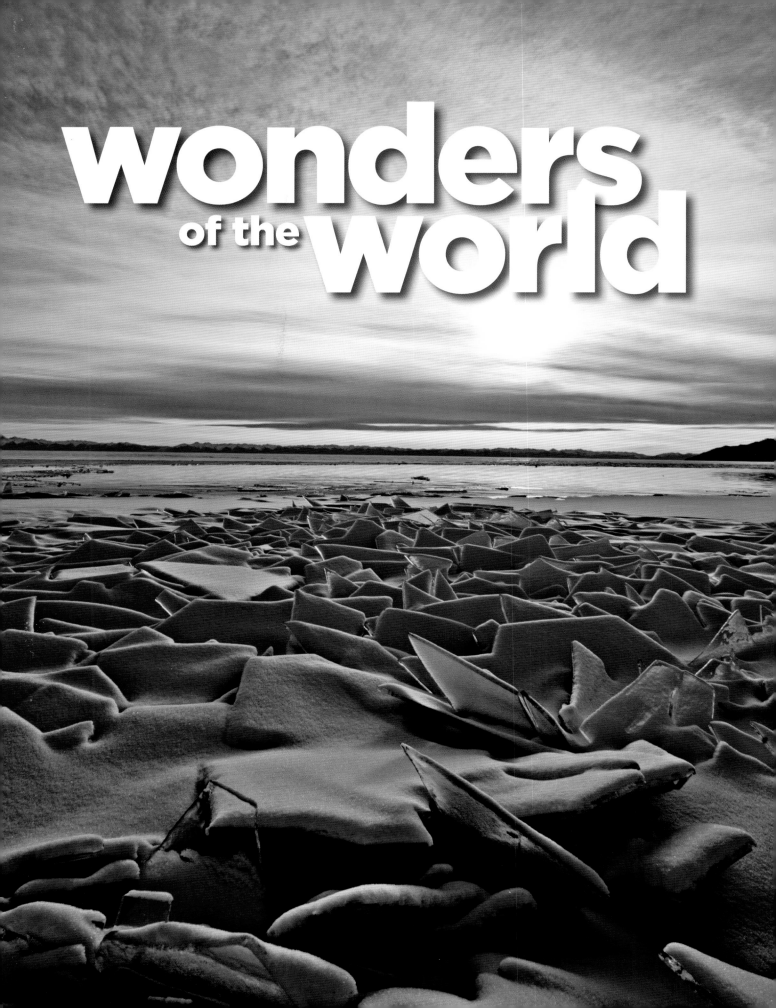

wonders
of the world

WORLD OF EXTREMES

The planet's dramatic history reveals itself in the world's oldest and deepest lake, Russia's Baikal (previous page), and in the ancient rocks of Africa's Great Rift Valley.

wonders
of the world
Earth's most awesome places

NATIONAL GEOGRAPHIC
WASHINGTON, D.C.

SUNLIT SPIRES

Sky, land, and water all play starring roles in the dramatic landscapes of Patagonia. Here, eroded granite towers known as *cuernos* catch the light over Lago Pehoe.

CONTENTS

W

onders never cease, nor does our fascination with them. Marvels of extraordinary size, beauty, or strangeness transport us from our routine lives, commanding awe, admiration, or even reverence.

These are the emotions that stirred Herodotus in the mid-fifth century B.C. An indefatigable traveler, as well as the "Father of History," he wrote home enthusiastically to tell his fellow Greeks how exciting other lands could be. Today, these are the emotions that the National Geographic Society shares through its magazines, books, films, and television programs.

Since its founding in 1888, the Society has been providing "a window on the world" to armchair explorers. Much like Herodotus, the writers, photographers, and filmmakers of National Geographic are driven to explore the wonders of sky, earth, and sea. That sends them to the bizarre vistas of the Great Rift Valley in East Africa; to the depths of the virtually unexplored blue holes in the Bahamas; and to the highest point on Earth, the fearsome Mount Everest.

On the following pages 25 of the world's most awe-inspiring places and phenomena are presented under the headings Sky, Land, and Water. These places are products of geologic forces and biological conditions that stretch back millions of years. They still inspire us today, much as distant lands inspired Herodotus and, with care, will inspire generations to come.

TWILIGHT ERUPTION

Fresh-flowing lava outlines cooler rocks in neon orange on Tanzania's Ol Doinyo Lengai volcano. The Maasai know the stratovolcano as "The Mountain of God."

Solar wind particles travel 93 million miles (150 million km) before becoming visible as the aurora borealis.

ELECTRIC SKY

The aurora borealis, or northern lights, blasts through the sky above Crow Creek mine near Girdwood, Alaska. The red and green colors are produced by charged particles interacting with oxygen at different layers of the atmosphere.

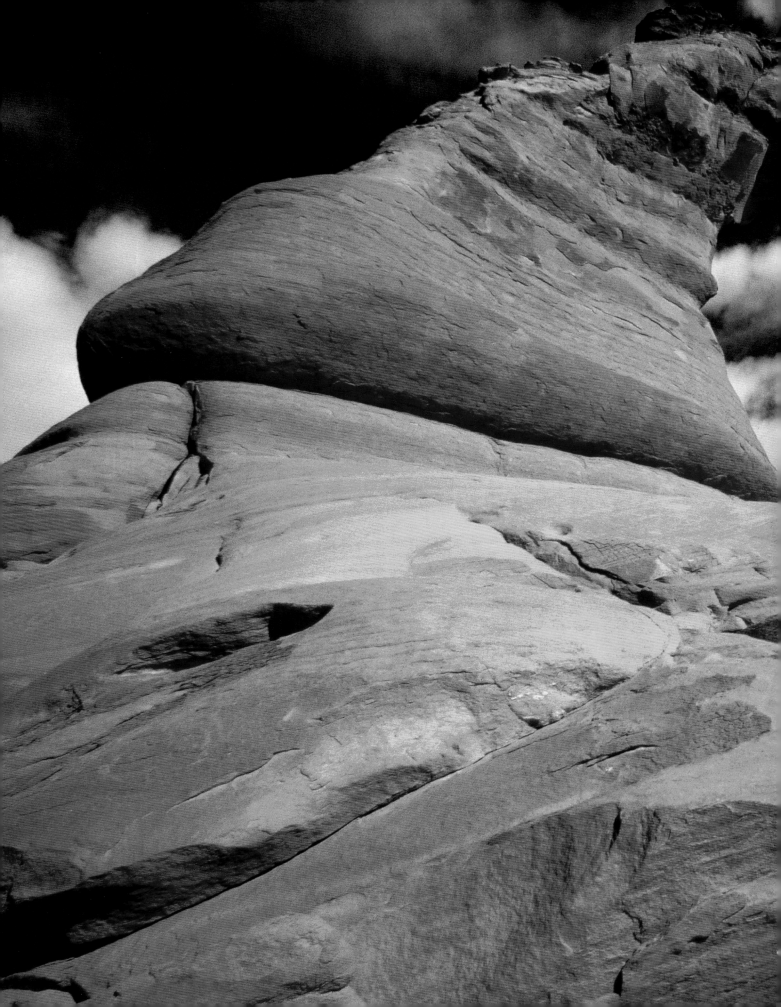

Sandstone arches reveal millions of years of geologic history.

SCULPTED BY THE ELEMENTS

The layered sandstone of Delicate Arch, in Utah's Arches National Park, is a testament to the shaping power of wind, water, and salt. Once covered by oceans, the hardened sediment has been exposed and sculpted for millions of years.

Over 98 percent

of the world's fresh water is found in glaciers and ice caps.

FROZEN ASSETS

Ice crumbling from the edges of the Perito Moreno glacier does little to reduce the size of Patagonia's Southern Ice Field, the third largest glacial expanse in the world.

Arctic Circle

NORTH

AMERICA

Arct
Fjo
No

Blue Lagoon
Iceland
p. 124

Redwoods
California, U.S.
p. 24

Yellowstone
Wyoming, Idaho, Montana, U.S.
p. 44

Kelp forests
California, U.S.
p. 98

Grand Canyon
Arizona, U.S.
p. 62

North Shore
Hawai'i, U.S.
p. 102

Cave of Crystals
Mexico
p. 56

Blue holes
Bahamas
p. 88

S
No

Hawai'i Volcanoes
Hawai'i, U.S.
p. 52

Underwater sculpture garden
Grenada
p. 106

A

Pacific

A
t
l
a
n
t
i
c

Ocean

Machu Picchu
Peru
p. 28

SOUTH

AMERICA

O
c
e
a
n

Altiplano
Bolivia, Peru, Argentina
p. 20

Patagonia
Argentina, Chile
p. 72

world of
wonders

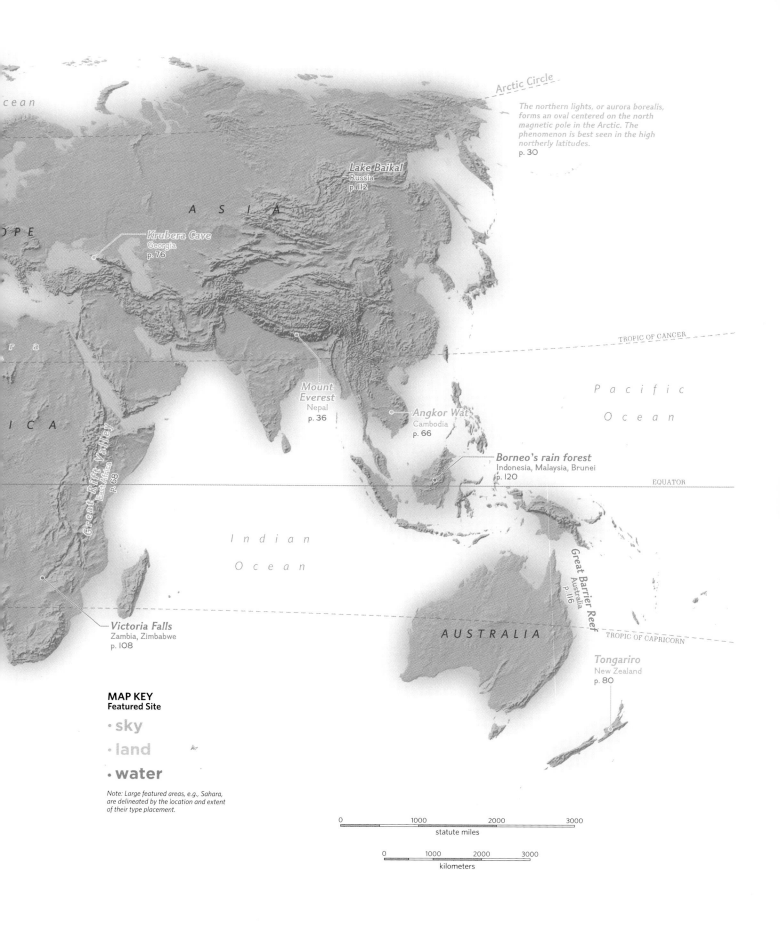

Arctic Circle

The northern lights, or aurora borealis, forms an oval centered on the north magnetic pole in the Arctic. The phenomenon is best seen in the high northerly latitudes.
p. 30

Lake Baikal
Russia
p. 112

A S I A

Krubera Cave
Georgia
p. 76

OPE

ra

TROPIC OF CANCER

Pacific

Ocean

Mount Everest
Nepal
p. 36

Angkor Wat
Cambodia
p. 66

ICA

Borneo's rain forest
Indonesia, Malaysia, Brunei
p. 120

Great Rift Valley
East Africa
p. 68

EQUATOR

Indian

Ocean

Great Barrier Reef
Australia
p. 116

Victoria Falls
Zambia, Zimbabwe
p. 108

AUSTRALIA

TROPIC OF CAPRICORN

Tongariro
New Zealand
p. 80

MAP KEY
Featured Site

• sky

• land

• water

Note: Large featured areas, e.g., Sahara, are delineated by the location and extent of their type placement.

| 0 | 1000 | 2000 | 3000 |
statute miles

| 0 | 1000 | 2000 | 3000 |
kilometers

SKY

WALKING IN THE AIR

The air is thin, but the views are incomparable atop Bolivia's Mount Sajama (21,463 feet/6,542 m). The extinct volcano is the country's highest peak.

The world's
highest
reaches

"When I follow the serried multitude of the stars in their circular course, my feet no longer touch the earth." —*Ptolemy*

When we raise our eyes from the ground and see the sky—or when we stand high above the world and look down upon the clouds—we feel ourselves lifted to another level of existence. We so clearly belong to the earth that to experience life at the heights is to become something else entirely, less human and more celestial. Even when the sky is frightening it is, quite truly, uplifting.

This may explain, at least in part, why we are awed by and attracted to high places, and also to those plants, animals, and natural features that make their homes in the sky. To see the world's highest reaches means stepping out of our earthbound skins for a little while. The redwood tree is impressive not just for sheer size or age, but also because it overtops all other living things. The high plateau of Bolivia and the secluded reaches of Machu Picchu take us into a realm few people have known, one of keening winds and huge-winged, soaring birds. Mount Everest, lure and bane of so many a climber, gives humans a God's-eye view, a perspective they know they were not born to experience. And perhaps the most breathtaking of all, the northern lights, take our familiar night sky and make it dance. Suddenly we realize we are just tiny beings on a planet surrounded by crackling energies. Reaching into the heights means entering into a fantasy world where we shed our human forms and briefly know what it is to fly.

SHEER IMMENSITY

A string of climbers makes its way across the sheer sides of the Karakoram Range's K2 (28,251 feet/8,611 m), the second highest mountain in the world. Known as the Savage Mountain, it is one of the most dangerous destinations on Earth.

ALTIPLANO

A landscape of ice, fire, wind and salt stretching

600 miles

(965 km)

BOLIVIA, PERU, AND ARGENTINA Rich in silver, salt, and eerie appeal, the altiplano holds a mirror to the sky. The 12,000-foot-high (3,660 m) plateau stretches 600 miles (965 km) through the Andes of Bolivia, Peru, and Argentina, one of Earth's largest tablelands. The water basins that once covered it have evaporated, but it still holds Titicaca, the world's highest navigable lake. Bolivia's capital, La Paz, is in the wetter north. The dry, lonely south includes Salar de Uyuni, an otherworldly saltscape; Laguna Colorada, a salty, reddish lake favored by flamingos; and the sulfurous mudpots of Sol de Mañana. There's silver and tin beneath the surface, but few trees survive in the wind-sheared expanses and few crops can be coaxed from the ground.

BLUE HORIZONS

A herd of domesticated llamas stands out in relief on the flat, spring-fed pastures of the altiplano. Llamas and alpacas are native to the high, windswept region.

SKY

FINE FEATHERED FAMILIES

Reflected in Laguna Colorada's quiet waters, puna (or James's) flamingos tend their less colorful young. The unusual birds are found only on high Andean plateaus.

REDWOODS

The tallest redwood measures

379.1 feet (115.5 m).

CALIFORNIA Much about a redwood is impressive, especially its size (up to 379.1 feet/115.5 m) and life span (up to 2,000 years; its scientific name *sempervirens* means "living forever"). These magnificent trees once covered two million acres along the Pacific coast of California and Oregon, but their valuable timber was heavily logged in the 19th century. This destroyed 96 percent of the old-growth forest. What remains in California's Redwood National and State Parks is still the world's tallest forest.

Redwoods thrive in a limited range of conditions. They can't grow directly along the coast because they are vulnerable to salt spray. Yet they must be close enough to the ocean that fog can condense on them on summer nights, providing vital moisture during the dry season.

A NATURAL CATHEDRAL

Redwoods reach for the sky—and for the life-sustaining moisture of fog—in Prairie Creek Redwoods State Park, California. The old-growth trees are part of an international biosphere reserve.

REDWOODS

LIFE AT THE TOP

On average, redwoods can reach heights of 300 feet (91 m). Rising even higher is the 365.5-foot (111.4 m) coast redwood, named the National Geographic Society Tree, one of the world's tallest.

MACHU PICCHU

Almost 8,000 feet (2,438 m) above sea level

PERU   On a drizzly July morning in 1911, Peruvian guides led American explorer Hiram Bingham through dense mountain vegetation and into a wonder. "We found ourselves in the midst of a tropical forest, beneath the shade of whose trees we could make out a maze of ancient walls," he wrote. Soon to be famous to the wider world as Machu Picchu, the pre-Columbian Inca site—with its dry-stone walls, terraces, and ramps—has since been partially cleared and restored.

The Historic Sanctuary of Machu Picchu extends out from the ruins themselves to include the remarkable, lush plants that swathe the 7,970-foot-high (2,430 m) site. In the humid forest, ferns, palms, begonias, and hundreds of species of orchids abound. The sanctuary, which is almost surrounded by the Rio Urubamba, also provides a home for animals including ocelots, otters, spectacled bears, and Andean condors.

SACRED CITY OF STONE

(Clockwise from top left) Machu Picchu as it appears today, on a ridge above the Urubamba Valley; expertly crafted drystone houses and steps; typical trapezoidal windows; a view of the site in 1911. Archaeologists believe the setting was sacred to the Inca.

SKY

NORTHERN LIGHTS

The aurora borealis forms a **2,000 mile-wide** (3,219 km) oval over the North Pole.

ARCTIC CIRCLE The northern lights, or aurora borealis, forms in the roiling interior of the sun. The atoms that make up solar gases are transformed into a thin stream of electrically charged particles—protons and electrons. This stream, the solar wind, is both matter and energy. It continuously erupts from the sun. Most of the solar wind sideswipes the Earth's magnetic shield, but some spirals down toward the planet's north and south magnetic poles, where it churns the oxygen and nitrogen in the atmosphere. Shades of green, red, bright pink, blue, or violet appear depending on how far from Earth the electrons and nitrogen molecules interact.

AN AUDIENCE OF ONE

Residents of Alaska, such as this woman in Anchorage, know that the best time to view the northern lights is during long midwinter nights, when the sun is at "solar maximum"—the period of greatest activity in the solar cycle.

DANCING LIGHTS

Auroral displays swirl in the skies above Alaska's Portage Lake (left) and Bleik, Norway (right). Greenish-white is the most typical auroral color.

NORTHERN LIGHTS

CELESTIAL FIREWORKS

Colliding with atmospheric gases, charged solar particles create an infinite variety of auroral displays. Variations in altitude, type of gas, intensity of solar wind, and position of the observer affect the appearance of an aurora.

The Northern Lights

The ever changing dance of lights belies the aurora's permanence. Though only parts of it can be seen at any time, the aurora borealis forms a 2,000-mile-wide (3,219 km) auroral oval above the magnetic north pole every day.

The Earth's magnetic field forms a protective envelope called the magnetosphere. Arriving with great force, the solar wind compresses the front end of the magnetosphere and elongates the back end into a tail ①. At the point of impact, if properly aligned, the solar wind's magnetic field ② links up with magnetic field lines from Earth ③. This connection produces the auroras seen on dark winter days in the extreme north and south latitudes ④. As it blows by the Earth, the solar wind peels back the planet's field lines now linked to it ⑤. When those lines reach the tail of the magnetosphere, they break away from the solar wind and reconnect ⑥. Scientists still do not fully understand how, but this process of reconnection transforms magnetic energy into kinetic energy, which then propels electrons and positive ions into Earth's atmosphere along the newly reconnected field lines ⑦. These speeding particles, especially the electrons, create the nighttime auroras. Crashing into the atmosphere ⑧, electrons hit the atoms and molecules of gases such as oxygen and nitrogen. In each collision, the atom or molecule absorbs energy from the electron, then releases the light ⑨. Color depends on which gas is hit and at what altitude.

MOUNT EVEREST

The world's highest peak stands

29,035 feet (8,850 m).

NEPAL Some 325 million years ago, Mount Everest was the floor of the ancient Tethys Sea. But about 60 million years ago, the tectonic plate carrying India collided with the Eurasian plate, forcing the ocean floor against the Asian landmass, squeezing and thrusting it slowly, giving rise to the Himalaya mountain range 25 million years ago. The grandly named Great Trigonometric Survey, begun by Sir George Everest in 1830, measured the mountain for the first time, and in 1852 declared it the highest point on Earth—a lofty 29,035 feet (8,850 m). It was not until 101 years later, in 1953, that Edmund Hillary, a New Zealand beekeeper, and Tenzing Norgay, a Sherpa, became the first people known to reach the summit.

BECAUSE IT IS THERE

Flanked by prayer flags, a mountaineer watches sunset light gild the top of Mount Everest from the vantage point of Gokyo Ri, in Khumbu, Nepal.

SKY

TOP OF THE WORLD

Mount Everest's summit (above), seen here from base camp, is frequently shrouded in clouds. At 25,000 feet (7,620 m), climbers press on toward the peak (right).

land

BLUE MOON, PURPLE MOUNTAIN

Looking as otherworldly as the moon that hangs near it, Mount Fitzroy in Parque Nacional los Glaciares, Argentina, presents a sheer granite face that is one of mountaineering's greatest challenges.

Land-scapes

that seize our imagination

"Land is immortal, for it harbors the mysteries of creation." *–Anwar Sadat*

We humans see very little of the planet's surface in our lifetimes. About two-thirds of that surface, of course, is below the ocean; of the remaining third, much is covered with ice, or barren rock, or uninhabitable mountains. Human settlements cluster around coasts and rivers and the flatlands that we have tamed and cultivated.

Our cities and our gentle farmlands have their claims to beauty, but the landscapes that seize our imaginations are those that reveal the elemental power of nature. We feel awe in places where the forces that shape the Earth are still visibly at work. We marvel at places such as Yellowstone, where an enormous caldera heats bubbling pools and propels geysers skyward. In the Sahara, we witness how shifting climate patterns took a swampy land, dried it into a scorching expanse of sand and scrub, and now are bringing greenery back to its edges.

In New Zealand's Tongariro National Park, sacred volcanoes rise amid waterfalls. In Patagonia, winds sweep across lonely grasslands backed by the cruel spikes of the Andes. Krubera, the deepest cave yet explored, descends into a limestone blackness that seems to take us back into the darkness of time. Even some of humanity's grandest constructions, like the magnificent temples of Angkor Wat, have been easily disassembled by nature. Although these places may be hostile to human life, they still enthrall us.

In these parts of the world, we can see the land forming itself on a grand scale, following its own natural logic, indifferent to our needs. We experience something greater and stronger than ourselves and know it as wonderful.

BEAUTIFUL AND DEADLY

As lava pours into the sea near Kalapana, Hawai'i, it raises a cloud of hydrochloric acid steam that reflects the lava's glow. The Kilauea volcano largely destroyed the town of Kalapana in 1990.

YELLOWSTONE

Yellowstone is home to more geothermal features than any place on Earth.

WYOMING, IDAHO, AND MONTANA The world's first national park—established in 1872—preserves the continent's largest supervolcano, the active Yellowstone caldera. Within Yellowstone National Park's 3,472 square miles (8,992 sq km) of stunning scenery are at least half of the world's geothermal features, including more than 300 geysers and more than 10,000 hot springs, fumaroles, and mudpots. The park holds the largest concentration of mammals in the lower 48 states, with grizzly and black bears, gray wolves (restored in 1995), bison, elk, wolverines, and mountain lions. The Old Faithful geyser erupts 17 times a day, propelling thousands of gallons of steaming, pressurized water about 130 feet (40 m) into the air to the oohs, aahs, and gasps of visitors.

LIVING COLOR

Colorful, pigmented bacteria rings Yellowstone's Grand Prismatic Spring, the country's largest hot spring. The sterile water in the center is a simmering 160°F (71°C).

ANIMAL AND MINERAL

Wolves, such as this male calling his pups (opposite), roam Yellowstone in 11 overlapping packs. Mineral terraces (above) form from dissolved limestone that rises through hot springs, solidifying when the water hits the open air.

THE SAHARA

A desert roughly the size of the United States

NORTH AFRICA   It is the iconic desert. The Sahara is the largest hot desert in the world, covering 3.3 million square miles (8.6 million sq km) of North Africa. Towering golden sand dunes roll across its midsection. Summer temperatures routinely soar above 120°F (49°C). The environment was not always so hostile. For several thousand years, from about 8500 B.C. to 5300 B.C., a wetter climate supported savannahs, acacia forests, and even swamps. Giraffes, hippos, and elephants flourished. When drier conditions returned, most of the animals and people moved out. Now, the reverse may be occurring. A more humid climate, possibly the result of global climate change, is bringing greenery back to the fringes.

SAND TO SAND

Sandstone spires reach through Saharan dunes in Chad's Karnasai Valley. Wind and storms are gradually eroding the rock formations and returning them to sand.

LAND

OTHERWORLDLY VISTA

A Tuareg strides across the windblown sands of Tassili-n-Ajjer, a plateau in southeast Algeria. Eroded sandstone formations and prehistoric rock art give the site great geologic and historic interest.

THE SAHARA

EVIDENCE OF THINGS UNSEEN

Three acacia trees give surprising evidence of at least occasional rain in the rolling sands of the Sahara. In groups, the tenacious trees can help stop the spread of desertification.

HAWAI'I VOLCANOES

Erupting since 1983, Kilauea has added nearly 600 acres (243 ha) to Hawai'i's south shore.

HAWAI'I Hawai'i Volcanoes National Park is varied, changeable, and literally explosive. Its 333,000 acres (135,000 ha) encompass two active volcanoes—Mauna Loa and Kilauea—on the southeast coast of the Big Island of Hawai'i. Like the rest of the archipelago, the island formed over a hot spot, an upwelling of magma that repeatedly punched through a drifting tectonic plate. The park's seven ecological zones, ranging from seacoast to alpine, shelter rare species such as the Nēnē (Hawaiian goose), 'Io (Hawaiian hawk), and Mauna Loa silversword plant. But the volcanoes put on the biggest show. Kilauea is the world's most active volcano, with ongoing eruptions that paint the sky like sunset at midnight.

FIRE AT THE WATER'S EDGE

Tourists' flashlights stripe the foreground as lava and a steam cloud illuminate the background at Hawai'i Volcanoes National Park. Lava from the Hawaiian volcanoes can reach 2100°F (1200°C).

KEEPING AN EYE ON PELE

An observer monitors the activity at Halemaumau Crater, part of Kilauea's large summit caldera. The crater periodically explodes with gases, ash, and fragments of volcanic glass known as Pele's tears and Pele's hair.

CAVE OF CRYSTALS

30-foot-long (9 m) crystals half a million years old

MEXICO   Some of the glittering giants of Cueva de los Cristales, or Cave of Crystals, are more than 30 feet long (9 m) and half a million years old. But humans discovered them only in 2000, when two brothers were drilling nearly a thousand feet (305 m) below ground in the Naica mine, south of Chihuahua in northern Mexico. Crystals embody order, with stacks of molecules assembled according to rigid rules. For eons, groundwater saturated with calcium sulfate filtered through the many caves at Naica, warmed by the magma below. As the magma cooled, water temperature eventually stabilized at around 136°F (58°C). Minerals in the water converted to selenite, molecules of which were laid down like tiny bricks over the millennia to form these massive crystals.

THE CRYSTAL PALACE

Protected by an ice-cooled suit, a researcher rappels into the Cave of Crystals. Unlike most caves, the Mexican cavern is extremely hot, warmed by magma chambers underneath.

TRUE SHAPES

Explorers clamber through the enormous selenite crystals that sprout from every surface of the Cave of Crystals. Scientists call the crystals' sharp, regular shapes "euhedral," from the Greek words meaning "true shape."

Cave of Crystals

For more than half a million years, mineral-rich water filtered through this cavern under Naica mountain, depositing molecules of calcium sulfate in orderly stacks. Heated by magma deep below and insulated by thick walls, the watery womb remained virtually unchanged, allowing crystals to grow to immense proportions.

TOP VIEW OF THE CAVE

— Giant crystal

⬆ Door

◉ Temperature reading

N   0 feet — 35
     0 meters — 10

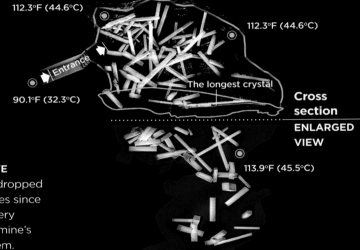

112.3°F (44.6°C)

112.3°F (44.6°C)

Entrance

The longest crystal

90.1°F (32.3°C)

Cross section

ENLARGED VIEW

113.9°F (45.5°C)

TEMPERATURE INSIDE THE CAVE
Readings have dropped about six degrees since its 2000 discovery because of the mine's ventilation system.

The Naica mine

Veined with ore deposits rich in lead and silver, the Naica mine would flood if the water table were not lowered by constant pumping. This action also drained the Cave of Crystals. The mine holds similar caves with smaller crystals, named for the shape of their formations: Cave of Swords, Cave of Candles, and Eye of the Queen.

Location of the caves

❶ Cave of Crystals
❷ Eye of the Queen
❸ Cave of Candles
❹ Cave of Swords

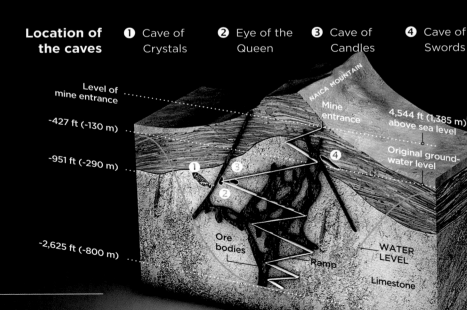

NAICA MOUNTAIN

Level of mine entrance

-427 ft (-130 m)

-951 ft (-290 m)

-2,625 ft (-800 m)

Mine entrance

4,544 ft (1,385 m) above sea level

Original ground-water level

Ore bodies

Ramp

WATER LEVEL

Limestone

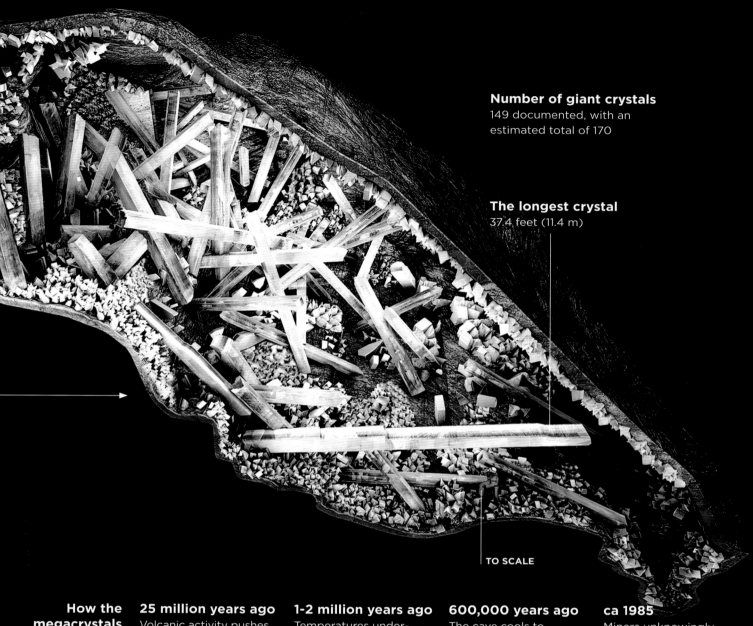

Number of giant crystals
149 documented, with an
estimated total of 170

The longest crystal
37.4 feet (11.4 m)

TO SCALE

How the megacrystals formed

25 million years ago
Volcanic activity pushes magma toward the surface. Intrusions of mineral-rich fluid will be transformed into ore bodies and mineral that later form the crystals.

1-2 million years ago
Temperatures underground decline and caves form, filled with mineral-rich water. Anhydrite, a type of calcium sulfate, begins to dissolve into the cave water.

600,000 years ago
The cave cools to roughly 136°F (58°C), the right temperature for calcium sulfate in the water to form selenite crystals. Undisturbed, it becomes a nursery for giants.

ca 1985
Miners unknowingly drain the cave as they lower the water table in the mine with pumps. No longer immersed in water, the crystals stop growing.

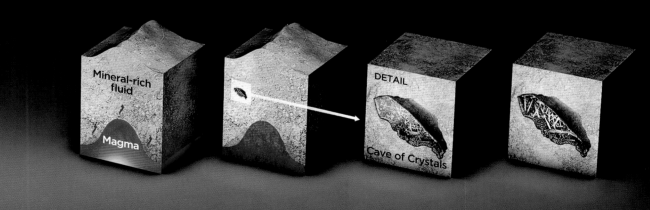

Mineral-rich fluid

Magma

DETAIL

Cave of Crystals

GRAND CANYON
The largest gorge
in the world

ARIZONA The Grand Canyon of the Colorado River is the largest gorge in the world—a gash that runs 290 miles (467 km) across the Colorado Plateau in northern Arizona. The Colorado River drops over nearly 200 rapids as it roars through the canyon toward the Gulf of California. A mile below the rim, the river slices through Granite Gorge, exposing some of the oldest rocks visible on Earth. Nearly two billion years old, the Vishnu schist is the gleaming remnant of a once-towering mountain range. Atop the schist, ten distinct layers of sandstone, limestone, and shale chronicle the advance and retreat of ancient seas, the building up and eroding of mountains, and the meandering of rivers over the years.

STORM WARNING

A storm pours rain into the Grand Canyon, feeding the Colorado River. Flash floods from rainstorms greatly increase the erosive power of the river, which runs a mile below the canyon's rim.

LAND

GRAND CANYON

SACRED WATERS

Richly hued sandstone and greenery frame Havasu Falls in the Grand Canyon's Havasupai Reservation. The blue-green waters are sacred to the Havasupai Indian Tribe.

reclaimed **by nature**

ANGKOR WAT

At its height, the city of Angkor was larger than Manhattan.

CAMBODIA In the 13th century, the magnificent Hindu/Buddhist temple complex of Angkor Wat symbolized Cambodia's Khmer Empire. Its lotus-shaped towers rose within a wall 2.2 miles (3.5 km) long. Outside the complex, the city of Angkor held 750,000 people, supported by a sophisticated array of reservoirs.

But by the 19th century, the city had vanished, its people had dispersed, and the temple complex had seemingly disappeared. In the humid, monsoon-drenched jungle, innumerable trees and vines had grown through the sandstone blocks and over the beautifully carved dancing girls, or *apsaras.* Among the worst of the botanical offenders were strangler figs, banyans that begin their lives as seeds dropped in crevices and grow downward as increasingly large vines that eventually merge. Off and on since the 19th century (interrupted by the wars of the later 20th century), archaeologists have struggled to clear the vegetation and rebuild the temple.

ROMANTIC RUIN

Enormous strangler fig vines have colonized the ruins of Angkor Wat (above left). Together with lichens and other jungle vegetation they eat away at the medieval stonework of the temple complex. Helping the temples survive are Buddhist monks (left and far left) who have maintained them for centuries and continue to visit.

GREAT RIFT VALLEY

A 4,000-mile (6,437 km) crack that began forming 20 million years ago

EAST AFRICA   Visitors to Kenya know the Great Rift as the breathtaking escarpments they pass on safari. Few realize it is actually an immense series of fissures slicing the African continent apart. Along nearly 4,000 miles (6,437 km) from the Red Sea to Mozambique, enormous cracks have opened up, as much as a mile (1.6 km) deep and 50 miles (80 km) across. In central Africa the rift has two branches: The Eastern Rift Valley bisects Kenya, skirting Mount Kilimanjaro and the Serengeti Plain in Tanzania; the Western Rift Valley cleaves the heart of the continent. The Great Rift began to open 20 million years ago, and the process continues. Experts say we could be witnessing the first stages in the development of a new ocean basin.

RISING FROM THE RIFT
Backed by Ol Doinyo Lengai volcano, Maasai warriors stride through the grassy plains of the Serengeti in northern Tanzania. The active volcano arises from the Eastern Rift Valley.

LIFE ON THE EDGE

The flora and fauna of the ancient rift region include (clockwise from top right) elephant families, herds of wildebeest, gelada baboons, and red algae in the super-saline waters of Lake Natron.

PATAGONIA

Patagonia's Moreno Glacier covers 100 square miles (259 sq km) and is still growing

ARGENTINA AND CHILE For sheer land's-end romance, no territory bests Patagonia. Covering 386,000 square miles (one million sq km), this wild plateau has some of the world's most pristine landscapes. Jagged mountains back cobalt lakes. Seemingly endless grasslands bend in the wind. Condors soar from the peaks of the Torres del Paine National Park, and rheas and guanacos run on the plains. Whales, penguins, and elephant seals swim off the Atlantic coast. Patagonia's ancient people, the Tehuelche Indians, were largely displaced by Spanish settlers in the 19th century, and even now the land is sparsely populated. Deserted highways bisect the steppes where an occasional gaucho rides by, evoking a fading world.

THE TOWERS OF PATAGONIA

The granite spires of the Torres del Paine, an Andean massif in southern Patagonia, were shaped by glacial forces and are aptly named for shark's fins, fortresses, and swords.

LAND

A FOX'S-EYE VIEW

Tucked within its tail, a gray fox looks out over the chilly Patagonian scrub. Though sparsely populated, most of Patagonia is privately owned, making wildlife conservation a challenge.

PATAGONIAN SUNRISE

Warmed by the light of dawn, ridged clouds cap the massif of Cerro San Lorenzo, the second-highest mountain in the Patagonian Andes. The 12,159-foot (3,706 m) peak is a mountaineering and skiing destination.

LAND

KRUBERA CAVE
The deepest cave
on Earth

GEORGIA It was "like climbing an inverted Mount Everest," one explorer said after descending into Krubera Cave. It's an apt comparison: Just as Everest is the world's highest point, Krubera is the deepest explored cave. It burrows into the Arabika Massif, a high limestone region near the Black Sea in Georgia's breakaway Abkhazia republic. In 2004, a team run by the Ukrainian Speleological Association set a depth record by reaching a sandy chamber, dubbed Game Over, at 6,824 feet (2,080 m) below the entrance. In 2007, another Ukrainian team dived into one of the cave's water-filled pits to a new depth of 7,188 feet (2,191 m). And when the exploration was over, the path out was a 7,000-foot (2,134 m) climb back up.

DARK DESCENT

Roped and ready, Masha Basovskaya prepares to descend another 330 feet (100 m) into Krubera Cave. The explorers rigged almost two miles (3 km) of rope through the cave's passages.

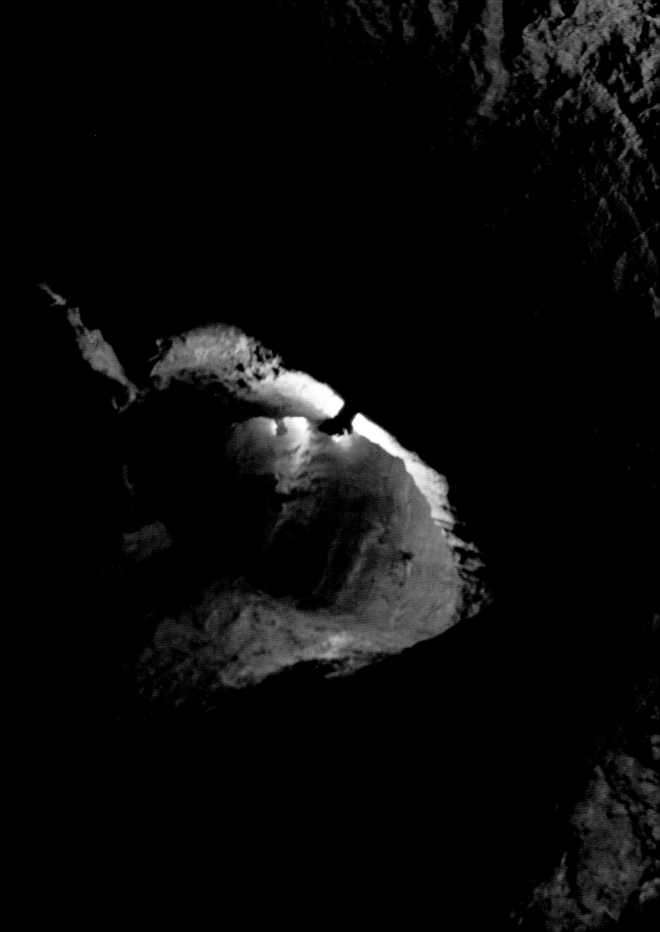

ELBOW ROOM

The Big Cascade, the largest pit in the cave, is 499 feet (152 m) deep but still 4,921 feet (1,500 m) from the bottom of the narrow, winding cavern.

TONGARIRO

Built by
250,000 years of volcanism

NEW ZEALAND New Zealand's Maori people say their legendary ancestor Ngatoroirangi was caught in a blizzard while exploring the North Island. Close to death, he called to his sisters to send him the sacred fire of their homeland. A blazing trail burst forth from under the island as volcanoes. Three of these peaks, Tongariro, Ngauruhoe, and Ruapehu (a location for Mordor in the *Lord of the Rings* films), now form the heart of Tongariro National Park, a natural wonder with spiritual significance for the Maori. The park includes waterfalls, emerald lakes, and misty fern-filled tracks. It provides shelter for native kakas (parrots), kererus (pigeons), and New Zealand's national symbol, the kiwi.

VOLCANIC EMERALDS

Smooth jewels in a gritty landscape, explosive craters atop Mount Tongariro hold emerald-green water, courtesy of minerals that leach in from surrounding thermal areas.

TONGARIRO

ON TOP OF MIDDLE EARTH

A skier enjoys the pristine conditions of Mount Ruapehu. One of three andesitic volcanoes that make up Tongariro National Park, Ruapehu is still active, periodically covering the snow with a thick layer of ash.

water

STANDING ON THIN ICE

Born on land, polar bears—like this one in the Svalbard
archipelago in Norway—spend most of their lives at
sea. Like almost all life on Earth, they depend upon the
delicate balance between ice and water, now threatened
by a changing climate.

water
Earth's great storyteller
"Water is the driving force of all nature" *-Leonardo da Vinci*

It's a water world, our planet, blanketed by an ocean, capped by ice, and carved by rivers and lakes and glaciers. Though it's all H_2O, water takes an almost infinite variety of forms and hues. The steaming turquoise pools of Iceland's Blue Lagoon, trapped in volcanic rock, present an otherworldly vision. Victoria Falls, thundering across a one-mile expanse, embody the sheer massive power of water plus gravity. The gigantic breaking waves of Oahu's North Shore tell of the power of storms at sea. And the sheer walls of Norway's crystalline fjords stand as reminders of the ancient grinding passage of glaciers.

Water captivates us not only with its manifestations but also with the life it nurtures. Around Australia's Great Barrier Reef, thousands of species make their homes, from dugongs to cuttlefish to poisonous cone shells. Drenched by monsoons, the rain forests of central Borneo are a biologist's fever dream. They hold pygmy elephants and flying snakes, not to mention the thousands of insects and mosses and lichens that form the base of the pyramid of life here.

Kelp forests off California's coast are rain forests of the deep, sheltering crabs and sea urchins at their base and rockfish and leopard sharks in their canopies. In some watery environments, we may even find clues to the shape of life on other planets. The blue holes of the Bahamas, for instance, nurture rare bacteria that can live without oxygen.

And as for humans: Though we are drawn to the water, this does not prevent us from polluting it. Sculptor Jason deCaires Taylor has created his own artistic commentary on the relationship between people and water in his submerged sculptures of human forms, gradually worn away and colonized by the sea and its creatures.

FALLING FREE

Long known to locals, Angel Falls became internationally famous in the 1930s after American flier Jimmie Angel crash-landed nearby. The Venezuelan falls, on the Churún River, drop free of the cliff face for 3,212 feet (979 m), making them the highest in the world.

BLUE HOLES

1,000 blue caves can be found along the Bahamian shoreline.

THE BAHAMAS   Inland caves flooded by the sea, called blue holes, are unlike any other environment on Earth. Reduced tidal flow results in a sharp stratification of water. A thin lens of fresh water—supplied by rain—tops a denser layer of salt water. The fresh water isolates the salt water from atmospheric oxygen.

Of the more than a thousand blue holes believed to be in the Bahamas, fewer than 20 percent have been probed. But the few explorers who have ventured there have brought back data that may deepen our understanding of geology, water chemistry, biology, and even astrobiology. By studying bacteria that thrive in these anoxic waters, scientists can postulate about distant oxygen-free planets and moons.

MILLENNIA IN THE MAKING
Divers swim up into the Crystal Palace section of Dan's Cave, a blue hole in Abaco, the Bahamas. The delicate mineral formations in this and other blue holes are thousands of years old.

INDIGO INVITATION

Dean's (opposite) on Long Island, Bahamas, is the deepest known blue hole, dropping 663 feet (202 m). The holes' azure waters lure divers, such as those exploring North Passage of Stargate, on Andros Island (above).

Blue holes of the Bahamas

SAWMILL SINK A blue hole is a flooded cavern with an eye to the sky, a sinkhole with a twist. Its opening, created by a cave-in, leads to a deep void and side passages filled with seawater. Conditions in this inland blue hole on Abaco Island make it ideal for reconstructing the ancient natural history of the Bahamas and can even mirror life on the planet billions of years ago. The cave-in that opened Sawmill Sink as early as 120,000 years ago filled it with a cone of limestone debris.

50 ft (15 m) wide

Fresh water

30 ft (9 m)

Water chemistry
An inland blue hole's water is very still and highly stratified. A lens of fresh water, from rainfall, floats on the denser salt water and isolates it from oxygen in the atmosphere. Brightly colored bacteria thrive where the layers meet (right). They need light but can't tolerate oxygen. Other bacteria here produce hydrogen sulfide, which the colored bacteria consume.

Sawmill's two side passages, each about 2,000 feet (610 m) long, descend as deep as 180 feet (55 m). Stalagmites and stalactites grow only when sea level is too low to flood the caves. Some formations merge into massive columns.

Debris cone

Mixing zone of fresh and salt water

90 ft (27 m)

Salt water

110 ft (34 m)

Stalactite

Stalagmite

Column

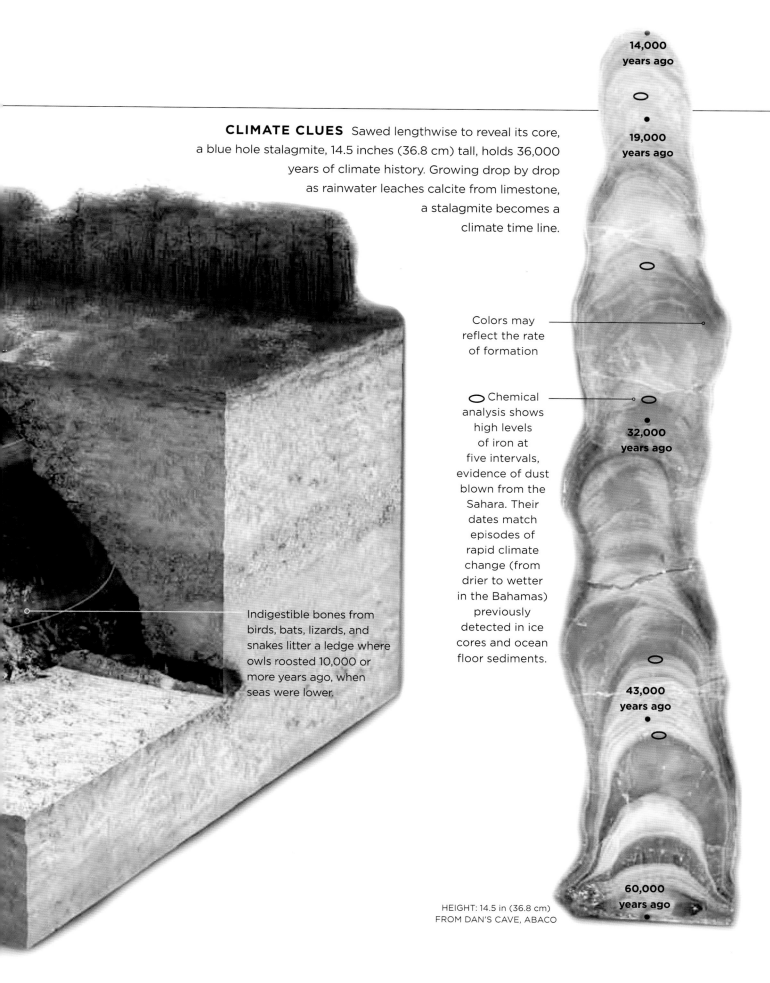

CLIMATE CLUES Sawed lengthwise to reveal its core, a blue hole stalagmite, 14.5 inches (36.8 cm) tall, holds 36,000 years of climate history. Growing drop by drop as rainwater leaches calcite from limestone, a stalagmite becomes a climate time line.

14,000 years ago

19,000 years ago

Colors may reflect the rate of formation

Chemical analysis shows high levels of iron at five intervals, evidence of dust blown from the Sahara. Their dates match episodes of rapid climate change (from drier to wetter in the Bahamas) previously detected in ice cores and ocean floor sediments.

32,000 years ago

43,000 years ago

Indigestible bones from birds, bats, lizards, and snakes litter a ledge where owls roosted 10,000 or more years ago, when seas were lower.

60,000 years ago

HEIGHT: 14.5 in (36.8 cm)
FROM DAN'S CAVE, ABACO

FJORDS

Fjords as deep as the mountains are high

NORWAY Gouged from Norway's west coast by glacial claws, the country's fjords are a spectacular by-product of long-gone ice ages. Over millions of years, heavy glaciers scraped U-shaped valleys deep into Norway's coastline. As the ice melted, the sea entered to take its place, filling steep valleys with salt water. Fjords can be remarkably long and deep: The Sognefjord, 127 miles (204 km) long, plunges 4,291 feet (1,308 m) below sea level. Steep rock walls typically frame the fjords, from which waterfalls arch into the water. At Geirangerfjord, no fewer than seven cascades—the Seven Sisters—plummet down one side of the valley, facing a single waterfall, the Suitor, on the opposite cliff.

HIGHS AND LOWS

Once occupied by intrepid reindeer herders, Norway's Geirangerfjord is now a UNESCO World Heritage site. Peaks around its sheer sides top out at 6,562 feet (2,000 m) above sea level, while the fjord's waters plunge 2,297 feet (700 m).

A HOME IN THE NORTH

Walruses (opposite), once endangered by hunting, are making a slow comeback along the fjord-indented coasts of Norway's islands. As lonely as they may appear, fjords such as this one on a Svalbard island (above) host a rich array of fish and other life under their mild, salty waters.

KELP FORESTS

A giant kelp
can live up to seven years.

CALIFORNIA Layered like terrestrial rain forests, from their swaying canopies to their shadowed floors, the giant kelp forests of the California coast are among the world's richest ecosystems. Cold, nutrient-rich waters feed the underwater forests, which consist mainly of two kinds of brown macroalgae: giant kelp and bull kelp. Each plant is anchored to rock by gripping holdfasts and held upright by gas bladders. They grow prodigiously—giant kelp can gain 18 inches (45 cm) a day—but they need light to do so and thus are not found below about 100 feet (30 m). Waving in the coastal currents, kelp forests shelter a variety of sea life, from snails and sea urchins to rockfish, sea otters, seals, and whales.

SAFE HARBOR

A harbor seal curls through strands of kelp. Many marine mammals, including whales, sea lions, and sea otters, find prey and take shelter from storms in kelp forests.

A LIGHT IN THE FOREST

In turquoise light, a diver explores a kelp forest off
Anacapa Island, California. Like land plants, giant kelp
need light to grow and so are found only in relatively
shallow waters.

KELP FORESTS

FLOTATION DEVICES

Kelp plants would be bottom-crawling vines were it not for their pneumatocysts, gas bladders that hold them upright. Giant kelp have one bladder at the base of each blade; bull kelp have a single pneumatocyst near the top of each plant.

NORTH SHORE

A 50-foot (15 m) wave

is as high as a five-story building.

HAWAI'I There are modest waves that lap at a toddler's ankles; angry, white-capped waves that keep small boats in a harbor—and then there are the colossal breakers of Oahu's North Shore. Located smack in the middle of the Pacific, Oahu sits at the end of an eastward-moving storm track. Over thousands of miles, storms from Japan build a swell that, in ideal conditions, will top out just short of the island's coast. The coastal shelf off the North Shore rises steeply, allowing waves to build rapidly without losing much energy. The waves that create the Banzai Pipeline on Ehukai Beach can present a face 50 feet (15 m) or higher, the height of a five-story building, to give a surfer the ride of a lifetime.

SURF'S DOWN

Two women surf the underside of a wave along the famed Banzai Pipeline, on Oahu's North Shore. The island's sharply sloping coastal shelf helps the big waves build quickly.

WATER

NORTH SHORE

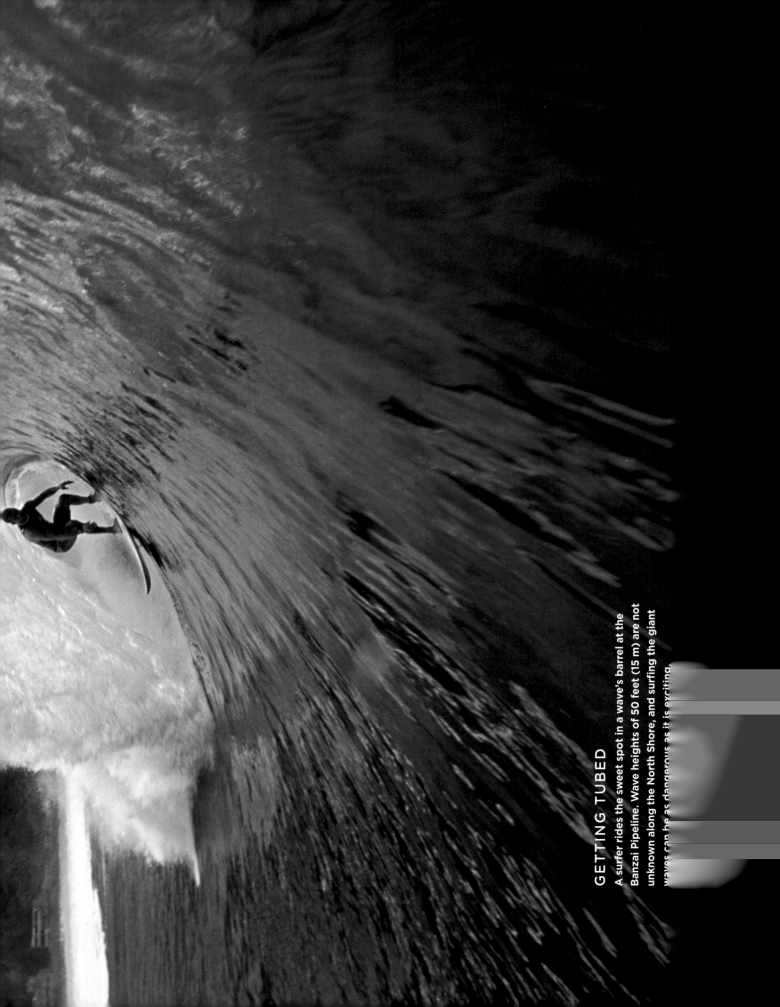

GETTING TUBED

A surfer rides the sweet spot in a wave's barrel at the Banzai Pipeline. Wave heights of 50 feet (15 m) are not unknown along the North Shore, and surfing the giant waves can be as dangerous as it is exciting.

GARDEN UNDER THE SEA

Sculptures morph into an artificial reef.

GRENADA   Twenty-six feet (8 m) below the waters off Grenada's coast, a curious figure is undergoing a sea change. Seated upright at his desk, hands poised before a manual typewriter, the "Lost Correspondent" is gradually but visibly being consumed by time and the ocean. This memento mori of the days of print is just one sculpture among 65 that British-Guyanese artist Jason deCaires Taylor installed on the seafloor of Molinière Bay, near Saint George's, Grenada, in 2006. A diving instructor as well as an artist, Taylor wanted to create objects that would respond to, and be colonized by, their underwater environment. The surfaces of his sculptures are treated to be suitable for coral growth, a process that will take decades. The mutable forms, as they become something rich and strange, will help rebuild Grenada's storm-ravaged reefs.

SEA CHANGE

Designed for transformation, sculptures in the waters of Grenada include (four images clockwise from top, far left) the 26 life-size figures of "Vicissitudes," 16 feet (5 m) down, and (bottom, far left) "The Lost Correspondent," 26 feet (8 m) down.

WATER

VICTORIA FALLS

The largest curtain of falling water in the world

ZAMBIA AND ZIMBABWE They were "the most wonderful sight I had witnessed in Africa," said Scottish explorer David Livingstone. Victoria Falls, which Livingstone named for his queen, were known more aptly by the local people as Mosi oa Tunya, "the smoke that thunders." Located on the border between Zambia and Zimbabwe, the falls of the Zambezi River are among the world's largest, spanning more than a mile (nearly 2 km) and dropping 355 feet (108 m) —twice as wide and twice as deep as Niagara Falls. The rainbow-infused cloud that rises from the gorge can be seen 12 miles (20 km) away. Narrow gorges downstream show earlier locations of the lip of the falls, which has been eating away at its basalt basin for thousands of years.

THE SMOKE THAT THUNDERS

In full flood, the Zambezi River drops 132 million gallons (500 million l) of water a minute over the 5,600-foot (1,700 m) span of Victoria Falls. The torrent is then funneled into a series of narrow gorges downstream.

WATER

FLIPPING FOR THE FALLS

Not quite as risky as it looks, a Zambian man's
somersault drops him into a pool alongside the main
cascade of Victoria Falls, 355 feet (108 m) high.

LAKE BAIKAL

25-million-year-old lake, 5,000 feet (1,524 m) deep

RUSSIA Russia's "Sacred Lake" is 25 million years old—the oldest lake on the planet. At 5,000 feet (1,524 m), it is also the deepest lake; it holds more water than all North America's Great Lakes combined. It is home to more than 1,500 animal species—including the only freshwater seal, the Baikal seal—and 1,000 plant species. Experts say Baikal is more biologically diverse than other lakes because oxygen-rich water circulates from its surface to its depths, a process likely related to geothermal vents. Deep below the lake's northern end, one vent provides warmth for sponges, snails, worms, and fish living in a pitch-dark environment. This vent confirms that at Baikal, continental masses are pulling apart.

SIBERIAN ICE

By midwinter, Russia's freshwater Lake Baikal freezes into clear ice at least 6 feet (2 m) thick. Well-insulated travelers can then cross the lake on foot or by dogsled.

WATER

FRESHWATER HAVEN

The lake's crystalline waters, fantastically deep in the center, grow shallow at the edges. They hold thousands of plant and animal species, many of them found nowhere else on Earth.

LAKE BAIKAL

SEDIMENTARY HISTORY

Baikal, 395 miles (636 km) long, has 1,300 miles (2,092 km) of shoreline. About 4 miles (6 km) of ancient sedimentary rock beneath the lake holds clues to the region's climatic history.

GREAT BARRIER REEF

World's largest grouping of reefs

AUSTRALIA Stretching for 1,250 miles (2,012 km) along the coast of Queensland, Australia, the Great Barrier Reef is the world's largest grouping of coral reefs. At least 2,900 individual reefs, along with some 300 islets and 600 continental islands, are sprinkled across an area of ocean larger than Great Britain.

This massive reef is all made of and by tiny, simple organisms. Coral polyps are tentacled animals with protective limestone skeletons. Dead corals build up over millions of generations into reefs. Only the colorful, topmost layer is alive. The 400 coral species of the Great Barrier Reef underpin an ecosystem that includes at least 1,500 species of fish, 4,000 species of mollusks, and 240 species of birds.

LIVING COLOR

A rainbow of coral greets a diving marine scientist on the Great Barrier Reef. Living coral animals make up only the top layer of the reef; beneath them are millions of years' worth of skeletal coral remains.

WATER

GREAT BARRIER REEF

INFINITE VARIETY
The reef is home to the quick and the dead, including (clockwise from top left) shipwrecks, crescent-tailed bigeyes, humphead wrasse, and broccoli coral.

RAIN FOREST

The oldest rain forest on Earth

BORNEO The tropical rain forest does not get any rainier than on the island of Borneo. Covering hundreds of thousands of square miles across the borders of Brunei, Indonesia, and Malaysia, Borneo's rain forest is pounded by up to 160 inches (406 cm) of monsoon per year. The montane and lowland forests protect a dizzying array of plants and animals, including orangutans, pygmy elephants, and the Sumatran rhinoceros. A single dipterocarp tree can host 1,000 kinds of insects. And the count has just begun. Since 2007, more than 120 new species have been found, among them the world's longest insect (a stick insect 1.6 feet, or 0.5 m, long) and a colorful "ninja slug" that shoots hormonal darts into its mate.

HONK IF YOU LOVE HORNBILLS

More than 380 bird species make their homes in Borneo's rich rain forests. One of the most spectacular is the rhinoceros hornbill, whose colorful casque, a hollow keratin structure on its bill, amplifies its harsh honking call.

WATER

TAKING THE LEAP

An infant holds tight as a proboscis monkey leaps toward a hanging vine. The endangered monkeys are one of 13 primate species found on Borneo, ranging from orangutans to slow lorises.

BLUE LAGOON

Seawater from 6,500 feet
(1,981 m)
below the surface feeds into the lagoon.

ICELAND Iceland straddles the Mid-Atlantic Ridge, where the North American and Eurasian tectonic plates are pulling apart. Upwelling magma built the island and heats its vast reservoirs of water, creating a geothermal paradise. First among the country's many simmering geothermal pools is the Blue Lagoon, a turquoise vision in a black basaltic moonscape. The geothermal spa is fed by seawater 6,500 feet (1,981 m) beneath the surface, where it reaches a searing 464°F (240°C). Capturing silica and other minerals on its way to the surface, it emerges from the ground at a balmy 100°F (38°C), just right for pampering visitors.

BLUE OASIS

The Blue Lagoon's intense color comes from a combination of blue-green algae and white silica mud. Visitors often rub the chalky mud into their skin, believing it has healthful properties.

BLUE LAGOON

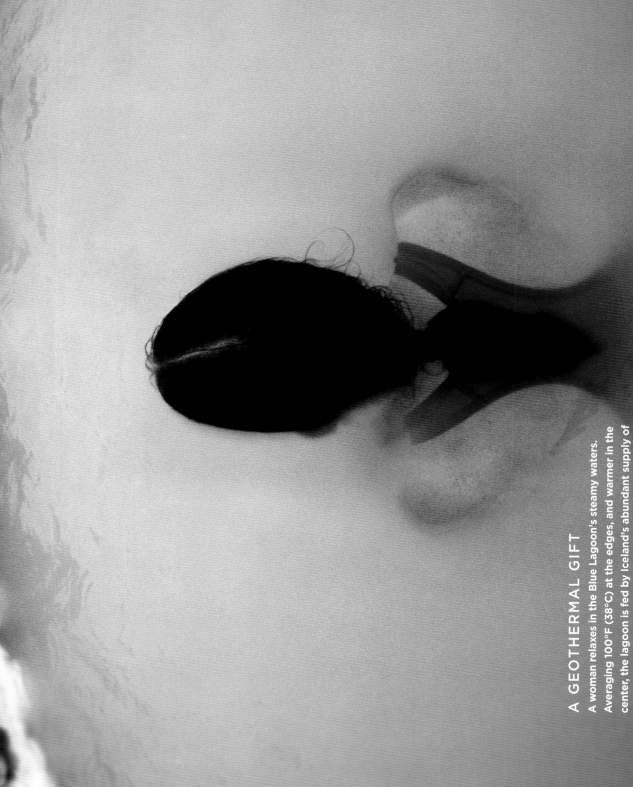

A GEOTHERMAL GIFT

A woman relaxes in the Blue Lagoon's steamy waters. Averaging 100°F (38°C) at the edges, and warmer in the center, the lagoon is fed by Iceland's abundant supply of heated groundwater.

WONDERS OF THE WORLD EARTH'S MOST AWESOME PLACES

Produced by the National Geographic Society
1145 17th Street N.W.
Washington, D.C. 20036-4688 U.S.A.

John M. Fahey, Jr., *Chairman of the Board and Chief Executive Officer*
Timothy T. Kelly, *President*
Declan Moore, *Executive Vice President; President, Publishing*
Melina Gerosa Bellows, *Executive Vice President; Chief Creative Officer, Books, Kids, and Family*

STAFF FOR THIS PUBLICATION
Barbara Brownell Grogan, *Vice President and Editor in Chief*
John MacKethan, *Vice President, Retail Sales & Special Editions*
Jonathan Halling, *Design Director, Books and Children's Publishing*
Marianne R. Koszorus, *Design Director, Books*
Bridget A. English, *Editor and Project Manager*
Adrian Coakley, *Photo Editor*
Bob Gray, *Designer*
Carl Mehler, *Director of Maps*
R. Gary Colbert, *Production Director*
Jennifer A. Thornton, *Managing Editor*
Judith Klein, *Production Editor*
Lisa A. Walker, *Production Manager*
Marshall Kiker, *Illustrations Specialist*
Robert L. Barr, *Manager, Manufacturing and Quality Management*
Patricia Daniels, *Contributing writer*

Material used in this book is drawn from the following National Geographic Society books and magazine articles:
National Geographic books:
Complete National Parks of the United States, 2009
The Wonders of the World, 1998

National Geographic magazine articles:
"Deep Dark Secret," August 2010
"Crystal Palace," November 2008
"Call of the Abyss," May 2005

For more information about NGS, please call 1-800-NGS-LINE (647-5463) or visit us online at www.nationalgeographic.com/books.

To order this or other National Geographic Collectors Editions, please call 1-800-777-2800 or visit us online at http://ngm.national geographic.com/special-editions/special-editions.

ISBN 978-1-4351-5279-3

This 2014 edition printed for Barnes & Noble, Inc. by the National Geographic Society.

Printed in China

14/PPS/1